Dealing with Scruples

A Guide for Directors of Souls

Dermot Casey, S.J.

Dealing with Scruples

A Guide for Directors of Souls

Dermot Casey, S.J.

Roman Catholic Books
P.O. Box 2286 • Fort Collins, CO 80522

De licentia Superiorum Ordinis: Joannes R. MacMahon, S.J.
Praep. Prov. Hib. Soc. Jesu.
Dublini, die 21 Januarii, 1947

Nihil Obstat: Gulielmus Moran,
Censor. Theol. Deputatus

Imprimatur: ✠ Joannes Kyne, Bishop of Meath,
die 11 February, 1948

Printed in the United States of America
ISBN 0-912141-76-X

CONTENTS

Introduction 7
Nature of Scruples 11
Treatment of Scruples 37
Appendix 69

INTRODUCTION

If you are a person troubled with scruples, this book is not for you. Don't read more than this first paragraph. Doubtless you opened this book in the hope of finding in it some cure for your scruples. If so, you are coming to the wrong place. What you need is not a book but a good confessor to whom you will confess regularly and whose directions you must obey with absolute and childlike simplicity. That obedience will come hard to you. You will be tempted to think that your confessor doesn't perhaps understand your particular case fully, that his directions to you don't apply in all circumstances. Then maybe you will try a different confessor, but you will still remain unsatisfied. Now all that is simply leading you astray and preventing the cure of your troublesome scruples. You simply must keep to one confessor and do exactly what he tells you, with full confidence. Leave the responsibility to him. He has a special power and grace to help you aright. He is speaking to you on behalf of Our Lord Himself, so much so that if you obey the priest you are obeying Christ, Who said to all His priests: "He that hears you, hears Me." Besides that special grace to give you the right direction, your confessor has wide knowledge and experience in these matters, which you have not. He hasn't to explain to you all his understanding of your case. Take it that he does understand. Listen to what he tells you, and obey him exactly, disregarding any objections or doubts that arise in your mind. If you do that, then, quite apart from the

INTRODUCTION

cure of your scruples, which will inevitably follow sooner or later, you are already doing something that is very pleasing to God, something that is very meritorious indeed: namely, you are being humble and obedient, and that, in your present state, is what God wants of you most. So what you need is not a book—you cannot obey a book—but a regular confessor who will guide you. In your present state you are incapable of judging your own case properly. Your judgment is warped, for the moment. Surrender it, then, with unquestioning obedience, to your confessor. That is your only way to get rid of your scruples, but it leads to certain success. So take that way cheerfully. And don't just give it a trial—a half-hearted trial. Whole-hearted obedience alone will bring you the peace of soul that you need so much.

If you are a confessor or director of souls, then you are the person to whom this book is addressed. Your moral theology has taught you a certain amount about the scrupulous conscience, and you have had experience of meeting a number of persons suffering from this kind of trouble. Now these people, as you are no doubt acutely aware, are sometimes difficult to cure, especially when their scruples are of long duration. In cases in which your efforts to effect a cure were unsuccessful, you wondered perhaps whether the whole cause of the failure lay in the scrupulous person himself, who would not obey your good advice, or whether things would not have worked out more successfully if you had handled the person differently. Seeing these afflicted people, you would like to help them in the best way possible, and for this end you would like to have as scientific a knowledge as possible of the nature and treatment of scruples. The aim of this book is to afford you some help in this matter. It aims at giving some account of the psychology of scruples and of the method of curing them, as a

INTRODUCTION

supplement to your own theological knowledge of them and your practical experience and good sense in directing souls. Properly speaking, of course, there is no such thing as a psychology of scruples, but only the psychology of scrupulous persons. The personal, incommunicable element is not to be ignored, so that each case of scruples presents a problem which is, to some small degree at least, different from every other, and if general rules of treatment are described, it is to be understood that they must be applied with caution in each individual case. With this important qualification, it is true, nevertheless, that scruples are to a large extent stereotyped in form, and that there are some general well-established principles of treatment for all scrupulous people. Still, to know these principles in theory is one thing, it is another thing to apply them expertly in practice. For that, experience, joined to native good sense and the grace of God, is the only teacher.

PART I

THE NATURE OF SCRUPLES

The word "scruple" is derived from the Latin "scrupulus." This first meant a tiny pebble, which, having slipped into the shoe of a person walking, caused an annoyance out of all proportion to its smallness. It afterwards meant a very small weight, about 1/24 of an ounce, so small as to affect only the most sensitive balance. Thus the English word "scruple" came to acquire the moral sense of a minute reason or motive so slight as to affect only a very delicate conscience. We still use the word in this sense when we say: "This scruple does you honor," and "He is scrupulously honest," or on the other hand "He is a man without scruples." The other meaning of the word scruple, the technical meaning which concerns us in these pages, is an unhealthy and morbid kind of meticulousness. A scruple is then an exaggerated, unreasonable fear of sinning where there is in reality no sin. This groundless fear of sinning causes doubt and trouble of mind. The scrupulous person becomes a prey to continual fear of sin, past, present and future, in the most innocuous circumstances. He is afflicted with endless doubt and mental anguish, causing a confusion of his judgment with regard to what is lawful and what is forbidden, between what is trivial and what is serious. His morbid fear of doing wrong only obscures his judgment and multiplies his doubts, and these in turn increase his fear, so that he comes to take alarm from quite insignificant and unreasonable motives.

It is easy to appreciate the difference between this scrupulous fear and the normal fear of sin in a delicate conscience. People with a delicate conscience know well the evil of sin; hence they fear it greatly and shrink from its slightest approach. "Such persons know the various kinds of sins and can see clearly the precise distinction between a mortal sin and a venial sin. When they come to Confession their confession will be marvelously exact. They know what sins they have committed; they confess those sins; they are sorry; but they are untroubled. A delicate conscience is a beautiful thing and must never be destroyed. It is right and accurate and correct and is often the sign of high sanctity. A scrupulous person, on the other hand, does not really know what sin is, at least in his own case. He is always uncertain. He is troubled with incessant doubt. He cannot be sure whether or not this particular act is a sin. Or, if he knows that the act is a sin, he cannot be sure whether or not he was guilty of it. He thinks that he was guilty, but he isn't positive. He runs to Confession, he makes a confession that is filled with the retailing of sins he is not certain he has committed; and he steps out of the confessional dissatisfied, uncertain, in an agony of fear that his confession has been bad and that his sins are unforgiven" (Daniel Lord, S.J.: *Are You Scrupulous?*).

Scrupulosity, therefore, does not mean simply a great fear of sinning, for if that were so every holy person, since he has a great fear of sin, would have to be called scrupulous. Some ascetical writers define a scruple as an anxious fear of sin, inspired by an excessively delicate conscience. This definition does not quite bring out the special nature of scrupulosity. It depends on what is implied by the word "excessively." The fear of sinning, in other words the fear of offending God, is a virtue, and indeed a very necessary one, and however great this fear is it can scarcely be called excessive, provided it is joined to a humble trust in God's mercy and protection. The great fear of sin in the saint has its source in the love of God, and the fear is greater the more intense is this love. Furthermore, in a holy person the fear of offending God, the fear of sin, is a harmonious element of the personality, in no way disturbing the person's peace of soul, whereas the morbid fear of the scrupulous person is an adventitious, parasitic and disturbing element in conflict with the psychological personality. The same may be said of the other characteristic of scrupulosity, namely, the element of doubt, or anxiety, which is doubt joined to fear. There is nothing abnormal in doubt, for it is a necessary consequence of our finite human nature. The holiest and most well-balanced people may be, on occasion, distressed by fear and doubt with regard to sin and temptation, without being scrupulous in the proper sense of the word.

An essential point, then, is the particular *kind* of fear and doubt about sin which characterizes scrupulosity. What kind of fear is it? Eymieu states[1] that it is essentially an *obsessing* fear, and that scruples are just one species of obsession. The word obsession, of course, is sometimes used to describe a very simple phenomenon, bearing only a distant analogy to an obsession in the strict pathological sense. For instance, when a tune keeps haunting us, we say we are obsessed by it, because it sticks in our mind in spite of all our efforts to get rid of it. This is an "obsession" without anguish, disagreeable but not painful. In the strict sense an obsession means morbid and distressing ideas which are tenacious, which cannot be banished

---

[1] A. Eymieu: *Le Governement de soi-même. II. L'Obsession et le Scrupule.*

from the mind by any force of reasoning, and which cause mental unrest and torment. These obsessing ideas tend to enter the mind when least expected, on the occasion of some act which is of an opposite tendency. For instance, impure or blasphemous thoughts may come to haunt the person at his prayers or at the time of receiving the sacraments. The basis of all this obsession is fear of evil. But any evil, hence also a physical evil, real or imaginary, can arouse fear and give rise in certain circumstances to unreasonable doubt and anxiety. Thus besides religious scruples, the basis of which is the fear of sin, there are natural scruples or obsessions arising from the fear of sickness, of dirt, of burglary and so on.

Certainly in extreme cases of scrupulosity the anxious doubts tend to become quite obsessing, haunting the person's mind unceasingly so that he can scarcely attend to anything else. But this is rather a secondary element, an effect of the scrupulous fear rather than a constituent element of it. Furthermore, not every case of scruples shows the characteristics of an obsession. The central element of scrupulosity is fear of sin, and the essential point to note, as we have already said, is the kind of fear. Scrupulosity can be described as a morbid condition or state of mind which causes the person to fear sinning, for unreasonable motives. This morbid condition of the mind is a psychological weakness which makes the person unable to formulate a certain practical judgment concerning the morality of his own acts. He knows the theoretical truth; he can make the abstract judgment concerning the lawfulness or otherwise of the act to be done, the conditions necessary to make a serious sin, etc.—but to apply that to his own case, to make the concrete practical application, requires the intervention of his will, and this is precisely where the scrupulous person is weak. He can readily give assent to the judgment: "When one has told all his mortal sins in Confession, the confession is good"; but to make the practical application to his own case: "I have confessed all my serious sins," requires an effort of the will which is beyond his psychological strength of mind. He remains undecided, unable to come to a certain decision one way or the other, torn by doubt and fear that *perhaps* he has made a bad confession. He looks for reasons for his doubt, but can find only trivial, ridiculous reasons, since there are no real grounds for his doubt. He has sufficient reasons to make the certain practical judgment, with no valid reasons to the contrary, but his strength of will is wanting. His mind is colored by the fear of sin, and this fear is made acute by his inability to come to a decision without knowing exactly why, by his state of hesitancy and doubt. It is a groundless fear, a fear which has no reasonable motive behind it, and the scrupulous person *knows* this in his heart; but on the other hand, his fear is very real, and he is acutely conscious of his practical doubt. There must be *some* grounds for his fear and doubt, he says, and his mind is in a state of agonized search for these hidden grounds, fixing now on one, now on another insufficient reason.

It is this acutely anxious doubt, with quite insufficient motives for it, caused by the incapacity of the will, which must be looked for in the diagnosis of scruples. When a penitent shows great doubt, anxiety and even fear, concerning some matter of conscience, the confessor should not jump to the conclusion that the person is scrupulous. His anxious doubt may be a sign of sanctity, of an earnest striving after great purity of heart, and to treat such a person as scrupulous, to tell him to despise his fears as foolish and unreasonable, would only do him harm and hinder the action of divine grace. Even when such doubts and fears have no solid reason behind them, they are not on that account alone a certain sign of scrupulosity: they may spring simply from error or illusion, requiring only simple and clear instruction to banish them. As we shall see more in detail in the following pages, when a penitent is readily receptive of instruction and experiences little difficulty in obeying the advice and direction of his confessor, this is a sign that he is not scrupulous. A delicate conscience must be treated in a different way from the scrupulous conscience; the confessor must be ready to encourage reverently the anxious striving of a soul after greater perfection. At the other end of the scale, if in the immediate past the penitent has been very lax in conscience, his present doubts and fears may be well-grounded, being the promptings of grace to purify his conscience by a confession made with extra care and exactness. Here the confessor must be careful not to confuse proper remorse of conscience with scrupulosity. These different kinds of conscience, which require different treatment on the part of the confessor, have some superficial resemblances to each other, but with proper caution it is not difficult to distinguish them in practice.

All this shows that circumspection must be used in diagnosing a case of scruples. A confessor or director should know exactly what scrupulosity is and what are its symptoms. He must not form his judgment too quickly, from only one or two indications. However well-informed and experienced a confessor may be, he will sometimes be unable to make a sure diagnosis of scrupulosity the first time he hears the penitent, and then he will have to wait and see how the penitent reacts to the advice and direction he receives. If he is easily reassured, and obeys the confessor without much difficulty, then very likely he is not suffering from real scrupulosity, or at least is only troubled by a momentary bout. Neither is it sufficient, may we remark, if the penitent introduces himself as a case of scruples, for it seems to be a foolish vanity in some, especially among women, to be treated as "special cases," and these may easily persuade themselves that a previous confessor has subscribed to their erroneous self-diagnosis. So far from being troubled with real scruples, these penitents often show a singularly lax conscience in the matter in question, their imagined scrupulosity being an excuse to continue in some bad habit. It is in general a suspicious circumstance when a penitent asserts with assurance that he is scrupulous. The really scrupulous person will tend rather to refuse to believe that he is scrupulous. His anxious doubt is evident even here.

Bearing in mind these rather obvious precautions, a confessor will, however, experience little difficulty in diagnosing a case of authentic scruples. The subject matter of scruples varies, and each patient is convinced that he is unique in his particular trouble, but the general symptoms are rather stereotyped, and the psychological cause and nature of scrupulosity are fundamentally the same in all cases, making it fairly easy to determine the general principles of a successful method of treatment. Should this fact not stimulate every priest to learn all that is known about the nature of scruples and their cure? He alone, by virtue of his office, has the power to bring comfort and relief to these afflicted souls, who often suffer intense mental anguish and are a burden to themselves and to others.

Having defined scruples in general and said something with regard to their diagnosis, let us now investigate somewhat more in detail their psychological nature.

It is to be noted, first of all, that the particular subject-matter of scruples in any individual is really of little importance. In one person the scruples will be concerned with the Sacrament of Penance, in another with Holy Communion, or with distractions in prayer; in priests the scruples often relate to the celebration of Mass. In more chronic cases the scruples may cover different kinds of acts. The particular subject-matter will depend to a large extent on the person's general character, on his habit of life, his daily work, and other duties. The subject-matter of the scruples is only a center or nucleus around which the person's fear and doubt crystallize. The cause of the scrupulosity lies wholly within the person himself, the particular object on which the anxiety projects itself being determined largely by extraneous circumstances. This can be observed in the primary stage of scruples, when the person's mind is colored by a vague uneasiness and anxiety, a feeling of incapacity joined to indefinite fear. This stage, however, does not usually last long; the fear soon begins to take definite shape, being associated with the objective idea of some matter of moral obligation in the person's daily life and duties.

There are occasions with most of us when we experience something closely akin to this mental state. They are the times when the normal person, passing through a momentary phase of psychological weakness, due to some overwork or ill-health or a variety of such circumstances, finds it difficult to keep up to the strain of life. He worries then about small things which normally would affect him very little. He finds it harder to come to decisions. He must continually reassure himself whether he has paid his bills, whether he has been given correct change, that his hat or collar is straight, that he has noted the correct hour of his train, that the letter he has just posted has fallen into the box, that the lock of the door has turned, that the gas is turned off, and so on. One realizes more or less consciously at these times that the worry and, fussiness is mainly subjective, especially as the mood passes quickly.

With the scrupulous person, the fear and anxious doubt

soon become centered around some particular class of moral act which causes difficulty to the practical judgment. Usually one general moral precept becomes the central idea of the scruples, and if the scruples become very chronic this idea may become an obsession: thus, for instance, "I am bound to avoid the occasions of such and such a sin," "I must observe the fast," "I must resist bad thoughts," or even, more generally, "I must keep in the state of grace." But whatever general formula becomes fixed as the guiding rule in the conscience of the scrupulous person, it will always be the expression of his greatest concern, the thing which is loved most and must be preserved at all costs and whose loss is most to be feared.

In most cases this general moral judgment is reasonable and true, but it is only the first part of the scrupulous idea. The difficulty comes with the particular application of this theoretical judgment to the person's case, with the proximate practical judgment concerning his own moral acts. "I am bound to confess all my sins in Confession," says the scrupulous person, and this is true enough; he is certain of that and it causes no difficulty. But he adds, "Perhaps I didn't tell everything." This "perhaps" is quite unfounded. The normal person would have sufficient grounds to judge with certainty that he had fulfilled all that was required for a good confession. The scrupulous person cannot just bring himself to make that decisive practical judgment. He will search out endlessly more reasons for and against, without ever finding certainty one way or the other. He will repeat several times the same confession with the greatest anxiety to be sincere and yet will be unable to rid his mind of that anxious "perhaps." "Reverence must be shown to consecrated hosts," says X, and this is quite right; and then he adds: "But there, on the street is something white; perhaps it is a Host; perhaps I ought to go for a priest, or warn the passers-by to take care." "One must avoid all occasions, of sin," says Y, and that also is true—but apropos of everything, a look, a gesture, a step, a bite, a word, he checks himself anxiously; "Perhaps there's a sin in that, or a danger of sin." "It would be a terrible crime to murder one's own children," says a mother who of course loves her children passionately—"But perhaps I have wanted to murder them; if I look at this knife, perhaps it is with the idea of stabbing them." Some are terror-stricken for fear that they will set a bad example and be the occasion of somebody else's sin. This can lead a scrupulous person into endless troubles. A man will begin to see possibilities for the misinterpretation of everything he says. A girl will begin to believe that her most innocent action is perhaps a temptation to others, a temptation for which she will perhaps be responsible. A priest will become afraid that someone in his congregation may be led astray through misunderstanding of his sermon. Then there is the person who can never judge with certainty whether or not he has fulfilled an obligation. He goes to Mass on Sunday; but, he says, perhaps he didn't give sufficient attention to the Mass. There is the story of a scrupulous priest who stood at the foot of the altar and gritted his teeth as he made his intention. He could not be sure that he had the requisite intention to celebrate validly. "Volo Missam celebrare," he would say, grimly, but his fears were not allayed, and soon it occurred to him that the word "volo" also meant "I fly." He would then say: "Volo Missam celebrare," adding immediately, "by that I mean volo-velle, not volo-volare"; but even then he was uncertain.

The scrupulous person is attacked by such anxious doubts, condemned to perpetual uncertainty, precisely in the thing which he has most at heart. He has only to desire this thing, to proceed to this particular action, and a chain of doubts and fears, a multitude of fantastic "perhaps," crowd into his mind. He feels that perhaps he has been at fault in this matter in the past, that he is running risks in the present, that the future brings danger, that perhaps he should make amends, take precautions, determine conditions. There is always this absurd, anguished and persistent "perhaps" clouding the practical judgment, and serving only to increase the feeling of fear. Each of these elements is necessary to constitute a scruple. If this doubtful "perhaps" is missing, there is no real scrupulosity, but only truth or error, as St. Ignatius says in the first of his Rules for Scruples. If the "perhaps" is not groundless, but is reasonable, we have a case of delicate conscience. Finally, to make a scruple, the thought must be tenacious; such thoughts occasionally enter the normal person's mind, but they are fleeting, being immediately evaporated by sound common sense.

Scrupulous people, whose judgment is obscured and afflicted by fear in the manner described, do not lack all good judgment. Outside the subject-matter of their scruples they can very often judge with prudence and common sense and can give good advice to others, and they may even be able to do this with regard to the very subject-matter of their scruples. Their theoretical judgment may well be unaffected, as we have said; the difficulty lies in the particular application to their own case, in the influx of the will to form the certain practical judgment. It is this particular incapacity which gives scrupulous people the appearance of being obstinate. They are not really so, and their so-called "obstinacy," their inability to be convinced by any persuasion of reason, comes simply from the fact that added reasons are no help to their will, which is paralyzed and weakened by fear. To despise their doubts, to act in spite of them, is beyond their strength, and to do so would seem to them inevitably to compromise the general moral precept or principle which is dearest to their heart and which must be safeguarded at any price. They become worried even by the fact of their scruples becoming less acute, because they take that as a sign that the impure thought or other temptation is no longer repugnant to them and that they are perhaps buying relief at the cost of surrendering to sin.

Scruples are a torture, because they involve the mind in a vicious circle of fear, and because they cause a blockage to the natural tendency of the mind and will which is towards unity of thought and harmony of thought and action. Scruples are specially painful also in that the persons afflicted are those who are naturally desirous of intellectual clarity, to whom doubt is specially repugnant, and whose wills feel the urge of striving after higher moral perfection.

The person afflicted with scruples tries to fight free from his anxious doubts; he brings all his reasoning power into play in the effort to argue himself out of his scruples. The unfortunate thing is that, left to himself, his defense against them is the more fruitless the more effort he employs. His mental struggles to rid himself of his absurd doubts not only remain ineffective but also aggravate his trouble. He is caught in a quicksand into which he sinks deeper the more he struggles to free himself. At first he will say: "This doubt is absurd. I mustn't pay any heed to it," but then immediately he will think, "I must; on such an important matter one must be sure"—"But I am sure"—"No, I'm not." Then he has recourse to reasoning. For instance, if it is a doubt about a past sin, every effort is made to recall the minutest details, in order to arrive at certainty; but if the memory is not clear and precise on every detail, this serves only to increase the person's doubt and anxiety. Had he a bad intention in that innocent act? Did he not think himself blameworthy at the time? Did he consent to the temptation? Did he confess the sin? Did he have proper sorrow and a firm purpose of amendment? Did the priest understand? Did he give absolution? Had the priest the intention to absolve? Had he faculties? A girl who is most pure finds a bad thought in her mind, and she rejects it in horror. Then she wants to be sure she did not give way to it, and she evokes the same thought in trying to judge whether or not she gave consent. This only serves to make the bad thought more vivid than the first time; she rejects it through fear of yielding to it and recalls it through fear of having consented, and she must examine it now for the two occasions instead of the one.

As regards doubts about the present, another says, "I am saying these three Hail Mary's as my sacramental penance; that is my intention now; it is for my last confession," etc., and in a quarter of an hour she cannot be sure what her intention was, nor whether she has said the Hail Mary's, nor even whether that was given to her for her penance.

These are extreme cases, but they are by no means infrequent. Those who suffer from natural, that is, non-religious scruples, sometimes think that they are on the road to insanity, and are reluctant to approach a nerve specialist or an alienist, because of the stigma of being thought "half-insane." Those with moral scruples are in a somewhat better case, for they will commonly put their troubles to a confessor, obtaining, if not a cure, at least some relief, and their scruples will be prevented from developing to extreme degrees.

"The fact of the obsession is quite clear to the patient—that is to say, he is conscious of it, and fights against it by reasonings, efforts and struggles of all kinds. Some sufferers make use of exterior actions to repel their troubles: they shake their heads or make gestures expressive of disgust. Some make their protestations aloud. 'No, never! How shameful! What an abominable thought!' and like expressions are heard from them. Or others will fall on their knees, and strike themselves—even hurting themselves—whilst they blame themselves and declare they must be responsible for their unhappy state. Many are constantly calling upon God, our Blessed Lady, their Guardian Angel, and the Saints, to whom they have a special devotion to obtain deliverance. Then others, again, are always making promises, vows and engagements. (Note: these patients usually make no distinction between a promise and a vow. The confessor should bear this in mind.) They impose upon themselves severe penances and long fasts, and deprive themselves of what is strictly necessary for them, and thus completely ruin the little health that remains to them, if they are not watched in a very special manner....These austerities only excite the nerves and aggravate the morbid state of the patients without any hope of ever obtaining the desired result" (V. Raymond, O.P., *Spiritual Director and Physician*). "The scrupulous find themselves ever face to face with sin. They fail to make any distinction between temptation and consent, between imperfection and sin, between venial and mortal sin, or between precepts and counsels. In order to give their attention to mere minutiae or to carry out some childish detail, they will not hesitate to commit some grievous offence or neglect the fundamental duties of religion or of their state of life. Some will insist on working when they ought to rest, on praying when they ought to attend to other duties, or fasting when they have most need of food. In the same person one may sometimes find scruples on certain matters and a total lack of consideration for other points of importance. For them there is no difference between what is essential and what is accessory. Conscience is wholly deranged" (Ibid. p. 105).

The exact psychological causes of scruples are not fully understood and we will not enter here upon a detailed discussion of them. Briefly, all physical and moral causes which weaken the nervous system and diminish the energy of character, especially when superimposed upon hereditary predispositions, seem to play a large part and prepare the ground for scruples. When circumstances cast the morbid seed into this favorable soil, the scruples will spring up, and the more favorable the soil, the more these circumstances can be commonplace. Usually, however, these circumstances which bring on an attack of scruples are such as demand from the person some exceptional mental or moral effort. Scruples are a sign of an "anxiety constitution." The scrupulous person is constitutionally prone to anxiety; he adapts himself at first more or less successfully to the exigencies of life until some greater exigency, entailing too great a psychological effort, causes him to stumble and to fall into the morass of scruples. This explains why many cases of scruples begin at the time of adolescence, a period of moral as well as physical puberty, when physical growth and adaptation to adult moral life require a more than usual expenditure of psychic energy. A similar effect is produced by other circumstances which involve a considerable change in life: the choice of a career, a religious vocation, a marriage engagement, a business difficulty, the responsibility of an examination.

Contributory causes are an unwholesome character training and a lack of correct religious instruction, which will inevitably induce the symptoms when the person's natural character is one prone to scrupulosity. What kind of character is predisposed to this malady? It is described well in the following passage: "The character of those liable to scruples shows a lack of resoluteness, and hence of determination of will in acting. This affords a favorable soil for timidity which keeps them from any social life and causes them to turn in on themselves.

These unfortunates, since they cannot appear or speak in public, live apart from others; and thus, because they lack the stimulus afforded by the approval or disapproval of their fellows become mentally and physically lazy. The disadvantages of this supineness is that they shirk the trouble of clarifying their thought or analyzing clearly their feelings. They live in a state of indecision; they never take the initiative; they have a horror of all responsibility. In spite of a normal degree of intelligence, they suffer themselves to be carried along without resistance whether the direction appear good or evil. With them kindliness and the absence of self-seeking are due to a rooted objection to any contest or discussion. Because of this need for a peaceful life they are most careful to respect the rights of others, so that their own may be respected. By nature, deaf to the call of duties of the moment, they are unpractical and live in a dream world indifferent to current happenings around them, they dwell among memories all the more readily since their imagination and memory are excellent. Disliking positive studies on account of the precision they imply, they are devoted to poetry, philosophy, religion; and let circumstances lend themselves ever so little to it, they indulge in a false mysticism, to which they are impelled by a turn for reverie coming from their inborn melancholy disposition. The affective side of these characters is richly developed. Feelings play a preponderant role with them, and lead them into every kind of disillusionment and suffering. Their emotional life, however, is so irregular as to be abnormal. The stoniest indifference is followed, without sufficient reason, by the most overwhelming regrets" (Arnaud d'Agnel et d'Espiney, "Le Scrupule," pp. 42-43).

The person afflicted with scruples frequently thinks his obsessing thoughts are temptations, or a sign of a sinful propensity, the "old Adam" trying to break out, and an inexperienced director of souls may make the same mistake. When an evil thought, born of fear, spontaneously arises in a scrupulous conscience, it remains for a short moment of time in sole possession of the field of consciousness, momentarily unresisted before the reaction of the will comes into play. This gives the sinful thought the appearance of a thought consented to, deliberately entertained in the mind, and the more so because scrupulous people often are unable to distinguish between thinking and willing, and do not understand that sin is only in the will. (Do not the very words, "a sin of thought," lead to this confusion?) Further, since every idea tends naturally to translate itself into act, the sinful idea spontaneously arising in the mind may cause initial impulsive movements. The scrupulous person, reflecting on himself, finds the sinful thought in his mind apparently unresisted at first and already passing into execution, and thus he is confirmed in his conviction of his probable consent to the sin. If he has doubts about his free consent he will be certain at least that it is a *temptation*. Now a temptation is the attraction of an idea inclining or soliciting the will to evil. The evil thoughts of the obsessed person come as we have seen, particularly at times of prayer, or at the time of receiving Holy Communion, and this gives them the false appearance of attacks by the Evil One. Scrupulous people are not, of course, exempt from sin or temptation—indeed they are sometimes very free and easy in matters outside their particular trouble—but they are rarely at fault or even really tempted on the point of their scruples. Real temptations do not take the form which we have described for obsessing ideas: bizarre, extravagant, monstrous, even more exaggerated at times of prayer and in proportion to the horror they inspire. With good-living persons at least, temptations do not immediately aim at very grave and obvious sins, still less at acts that are extravagant and ridiculous; but temptation goes straight to the satisfaction of an instinct, to pleasure for pleasure's sake, not to evil under the form of evil. The scrupulous person is assailed by extreme, monstrous ideas of evil with regard to the virtue to which he is most strongly attached. Here the will does not feel the least inclination towards consent; there is no temptation. Temptations attack the citadel of the soul at its weak point, its strong point is the breeding ground of scruples.

Of course, there is a form of scruples which comes as a direct temptation of the devil and which seems to be permitted by God for the good purpose of increasing the person's purity of conscience and humility. It is a painful but salutary period of desolation, which the soul must bear patiently, humbly and trustfully, being perfectly obedient to the spiritual director, and if it does this, it will emerge from the trial purified and strengthened. Even in this form of scruples, however, there is a difference from temptation in the ordinary sense, in that the scruples are not precisely in themselves a temptation to the sins they suggest, but rather an effort of the devil to lead the soul indirectly to disobedience and despair. The scruples themselves are not a sign of any evil propensity of the will. Even when caused directly by the devil, they will center more probably round a virtue in which there is no real danger of sin, and thus mask the astute designs of the Evil One. It is no unusual plan of his to appear to attack one virtue, when in reality he is trying to carry the assault in quite another quarter. In this book, however, we are dealing directly only with scruples which have an interior psychological cause, although of course the devil may also intervene here as an additional factor.

We have described the symptoms which characterize scrupulosity, and now it remains for us to outline the explanation of these phenomena given by the science of psychology, before passing to the treatment of scruples. Why is the scrupulous person afflicted by these fears and doubts? Why do these distressing doubts center round a particular class of acts, usually relating to the virtue which the person has most at heart? The efforts of the scrupulous person to reason himself out of his doubts not only remain sterile but increase his trouble of mind. Why is this? These questions demand an answer, not merely from their theoretical interest but also with a view to a right understanding and application of the method of treating and curing scruples. As with bodily illness, so with a mental trouble we must know exactly what is amiss in order to apply the correct remedy.

Let it be noted, in the first place, that scrupulosity is not any form of insanity, not even the initial stage of insanity. It is well to reassure a bad case of scrupulosity on this point, for the fear of the person is sometimes made more acute by the suspicion that he is going insane. He may think it, without daring to express the unpleasant thought. His difficulty in discovering reasonable grounds for his doubts and fears may easily put such a thought into his mind, especially if he is told bluntly that his scrupulous fear is groundless and unreasonable. He half knows that himself, for the trivial motives which he adduces for his fears do not convince even his own mind. He will think: "My fear is real; but if it is groundless, what explanation can there be except that I am going mad?"—and this increases his desperate anxiety to search out some reasonable grounds for his fear. The very fact, however, that the scrupulous person is *aware* that there are no real objective grounds for his doubts and fears is enough to mark him off from the insane. The latter are convinced by their delusions, and do not see their unreasonableness, whereas the scrupulous person, by his struggles to discover some real grounds for his fear which will convince him, shows that he possesses his reason unimpaired.

Superficially, of course, and when the individual symptoms are considered in isolation, scrupulosity shows some resemblance to certain forms of insanity. The element of obsession or phobia, which is observed in extreme cases of scrupulosity, is an example, and has led a few authors to consider scrupulosity as a species of obsession characterized by doubt. This view, we have already remarked, leaves too much out of account the central element of fear, and relegates the scrupulous doubt to a subordinate role, besides overlooking the fact that scruples sometimes do not show this obsessional character.

There is an even closer resemblance between scrupulosity and the pathological forms of melancholy. Yet here again a deeper glance shows that the two mental conditions are fundamentally different. For one thing, and this alone, not to speak of other important differences, would be sufficient to distinguish them—the melancholic, while he also is oppressed by sadness and mental anguish, makes no effort to find valid reasons for his state of mind, he is not tortured by doubts, but he simply surrenders himself without a struggle, without caring why, to a vague and general state of depressive sadness.

The psychological explanation of the inner nature of scrupulosity which is by far more generally accepted today may be termed the psychasthenic theory. The following rather summary description is in accordance with most authorities. We will follow more or less closely the description given by Père Eymieu in his book, *Le Gouvernement de soi-meme. II. L'Obsession et le Scrupule*. The mental condition of psychasthenia, first described by Professor Pierre Janet, is to be considered as the essential subjective cause of scrupulosity. Now psychasthenia is a deficiency or weakness of general vital or psychical energy. The senses and all the other faculties—memory, intellect and will, imagination, and even the emotions—are all in good condition individually, but the unifying psychical force which organizes the whole shows a deficit from the normal degree. This psychic force, sometimes termed the psychic tension, is essentially a unifying force, directing and organizing the whole life of the human person from the vegetative level up to conscious mental life; for instance, at the level of consciousness it harmonizes all the data of consciousness into a unified whole adapted to concrete reality, and the degree of this unification is a measure of the psychic force. The psychic force may and usually does increase with normal exercise, but at any given moment it is of a definite degree, capable only of a limited amount of unification. The nature and number of psychological elements unified must be taken into account also, for some of them entail a relatively greater expenditure of psychical energy, and the greater the number of elements unified by a given amount of energy the lower will be the degree of unification. The vital or psychical energy has therefore two modes of application: it may be applied to a small number of elements and gain in degree what it loses in extent of work done, or it can deploy itself over a large number of elements, in which case the degree of unification is correspondingly lower.

Scrupulosity is explained by the theory as a lowering of the psychical force to such a degree that the person becomes unequal to accomplishing certain mental acts. The mental acts which are affected first and foremost are the practical judgments relating to some one virtue, or some one moral precept, since these are the acts which come hardest to the person in question, requiring the highest degree of psychical force. The impossibility of forming these practical judgments results immediately in a chronic state of practical doubt, essentially a subjective doubt, and therefore without sufficient objective grounds to make it appear reasonable to the mind. The doubt comes from within, not from any lack of objective evidence, or from the presence of real objective evidence to the contrary, and this explains why all the efforts of the scrupulous person to resolve his doubt by new evidence remain fruitless. His very mental struggles, indeed, further reduce his psychical energy, so that he is rendered all the more unequal to the task of forming a judgment with certitude. At the same time this psychological incapacity produces the affective state of fear characteristic of scrupulosity. The practical moral judgments made impossible of accomplishment have a direct relation to exterior action, and what is more, to those exterior acts which fall under some important moral obligation. The feeling of incapacity in such an important subject matter will therefore be strongly tinged with fear.

The idea of a general psychical force or tension, then, is joined in this theory to the idea of a hierarchy of psychological acts of greater or lesser difficulty. The more the psychical force at the person's disposal becomes lowered, the greater the number and variety of psychological acts which become impossible to him. This phenomenon has been observed objectively. It ought to be possible, then, by observing a large number of cases of this psychasthenic condition, and noting what classes of psychological acts are progressively affected, to draw up a scale of these acts according to their degree of difficulty, and this has actually been done by Janet and other workers. The following hierarchical scale, beginning with the most difficult psychological acts and passing by degrees to the easiest, has been put forward by Eymieu as an improvement on that of Janet.

A. ACTS ADAPTED TO CONCRETE REALITY

1. *Moral* acts—representing the supreme adaptation to objective reality, comprising all the difficulties of voluntary, social action which has a personal interest for the individual.
2. *Voluntary* action of the individual on exterior objects and more difficult if performed in the presence of witnesses, *i.e.,* in the social as well as in the physical environment; and more difficult still if it is an unaccustomed act.
3. Acts of *attention* which are done deliberately and with certainty.
4. Acts of *memory,* fixing time and place, involving retention and evocation, *e.g.,* immediately bringing to mind all the memories useful for the present action.
5. *Consciousness of self,* with the sentiment of coordination, of unity.
6. Acts of *emotion,* adapted to present circumstances.
7. Clear *perception* of present reality, requiring attention and adaptation.

B. ACTS NOT RELATED TO PRESENT OBJECTIVE REALITY. (In these there will be less consciousness, less precision and less concentration.)

8. Acts done in an *abstracted* manner.
9. *Abstract* and *vague* ideas, *e.g.,* reasoning without certitude.
10. Acts of *memory* not connected with present reality.
11. *Associations* of ideas or images, day-dreams, etc.
12. Vague *emotions* not related to present perception.
13. *Tics, i.e.,* acts caricaturing previous movements, no longer adapted to reality.

It will be noticed that in this scale the various kinds of psychological acts arrange themselves in order according to their coefficient of reality, for psychological life is ordained to *action,* action on the objective environment. The higher psychological acts are those which are more perfectly adapted and related to the objective existing reality, and they become less perfect according as they are more divorced from this objective actuality. The more perfect acts, those higher in the scale given above, are more difficult because more complex. In this we have no more than an application of the general principle of Life, which works always towards unity in multiplicity. It follows that those psychological acts which are higher in the scale demand for their performance a higher degree of psychical tension or force.

The symptoms of scrupulosity show themselves when the psychic tension of the individual is too low for the demands made upon it. The doubt and indecision of the scrupulous person betray this insufficiency, because the conscious and deliberate act of *certitude,* in the particular subject-matter troubling him, is beyond the capacity of his psychical force. This insufficiency shows itself, first and foremost, with regard to those moral acts which the person has most at heart, because these are precisely the acts which demand the fullest application of mind and will and emotions, and which are at the summit of the scale of psychological complexity. This explains why scruples are particularly troublesome on such occasions as Confession, Holy Communion, prayer and other devotional exercises, as well as in acts of the virtue on which the person is most intent. The responsibility involved in these acts, and the very desire to perform them well, to give of one's best, greatly increase their psychological difficulty, requiring a higher degree of psychical force than the scrupulous person has at his command.

That is, then, the best psychological explanation that has been given of the nature of scruples. Its merit lies in this—that it takes into account all the known facts, according to their relative importance, and presents a working theory which is the basis of a successful method of treatment.

PART II

THE TREATMENT OF SCRUPLES

Although there is probably no case of scruples, however chronic it may be, which is incurable, the cure is often very difficult and very gradual. Except when the scruples are of a very mild form, their treatment by a spiritual director requires quite a number of interviews, spread perhaps over a long period of time, before a complete cure can be affected.

What can a confessor do, therefore, if a scrupulous penitent comes to him for confession on just one occasion? Well, there is very little he can do, and certainly he should not attempt the impossible task of curing the scruples by one interview with the scrupulous person. As soon as the penitent is diagnosed as scrupulous he should be asked immediately whether he has a regular confessor. If he has, it is most probable that this person is seeking a change without reasonable cause, just because of the difficulty he naturally experiences in obeying the directions given by his regular confessor. This is a very common tendency of the scrupulous. Continually tortured by their scruples, they will run from one confessor to another; they cannot feel sure that any one confessor fully understands their case. Their scrupulous doubt troubles them even on this point—"Perhaps he didn't quite understand"—they will say: "Perhaps the advice he gave wasn't quite correct,"—and so they will run to a new confessor. Now, this only makes matters worse, for even though the various confessors give the same advice, at least they will word it differently, and the scrupulous penitent will interpret these accidental variations as substantial disagreement. In addition, as we shall explain presently, the personal element is important in the cure of scruples; the scrupulous penitent must place his trust in one confessor and give him full obedience, not just the abstract submission to a doctrine or line of conduct, but a practical obedience in which human faith has a part. For this reason, it is a necessary condition of successful treatment of scruples that the penitent keep to one fixed confessor. Consequently, if the occasional penitent makes known that he has a regular confessor, he should simply be told to follow the directions which that confessor gave him, to keep going to him regularly, and to obey him exactly. That advice will strengthen the position of the regular confessor and help towards a successful treatment. Any additional advice would only be a disturbing factor.

If on the other hand the scrupulous person is found to have no fixed confessor, and if the present one is only passing, as for instance on the occasion of a Mission or a Retreat, the penitent should be made to promise to choose one confessor to whom he will go regularly for Confession. Here his scruples may intervene to make such a choice difficult for him, and it would be very useful to help him in the matter by eliciting the name of some priest to whom he would be willing to go, saying: "There now, take that as fixed definitely; go regularly to him for Confession, and follow his directions exactly; in that way you will get rid of those troubles." Once again, any additional advice would be dangerous, unless the scruples are seen to be very mild and passing.

Only when the scrupulous person can be made to promise to come back regularly should a confessor proceed to give further advice on the matter of the scruples. In the following pages, in which we describe how scruples can be successfully treated, we presume that this is the case, that the penitent returns regularly to the same confessor. The penitent can be encouraged to do so, by being assured that this is necessary for his cure, and that if he does so his cure is certain. Most moral theologians and ascetical writers go so far as to say that a penitent with very chronic scruples should be definitely forbidden to go to any other confessor. This is quite understandable and reasonable, given the peculiar nature of scrupulosity, the disimprovement which results from changing about from one confessor to another, and the necessity of enlisting gradually the penitent's complete confidence and obedience.

We saw in Part I that scrupulosity consists essentially in a psychological insufficiency, a psychical tension or force too low for the acts to be performed, these acts being in particular certain moral practical judgments. The logical method of cure, therefore, will consist in reducing the difficulty of the acts, or raising the psychical force, until the two are in proportion to one another. Left to his own resources, the person afflicted with scruples will inevitably fail in all this; all his efforts merely result in making more complex and more difficult the psychological acts in question and in further reducing his psychical force, accentuating the disproportion between them. He is like a person held fast in a treacherous quicksand, whose struggles make him sink deeper, and who can be rescued only by other hands. But while he must be thrown a rope, he must himself catch hold of it and not let go until he is drawn out of his difficulties. The cooperation of the scrupulous patient is an integral part of the treatment, and his confessor or director may need some personal genius in order to elicit this cooperation.

The fundamental and general rule for the director is that he must inspire *confidence* and require *obedience*. We say this is a rule for the director, by which we mean that it is something he must do himself, not a mere prerequisite which he must be granted in order to begin the work of directing the scrupulous person. The director will have won half the battle, indeed, when he has obtained the confidence and willing obedience of his penitent, but this half of the battle has to be fought by the director himself. To give up, therefore, at the first sign of disobedience, and to throw the whole blame for failure on one's penitent, saying: "This person simply refuses to be cured!" is to misunderstand the nature of scrupulosity and the director's function. Although scrupulous people feel the need of placing their trust in another person, in someone who will supply for their own lack of decision and psychological insufficiency, the placing of full trust in another is difficult for them. This very act involves a decision which is often beyond their powers, until it is made easier for them. Thus their scruples poison even their conscious need of trusting and obeying their director— "Perhaps it would be wrong; perhaps he hasn't understood my case fully." But their greatest obstacle to giving complete trust and obedience is their particular fear of sinning, the fear of compromising the general moral precept which is the focal point of their scrupulosity. They would surrender all else, if they were still allowed to use their own judgment on that. "Men especially," says Eymieu, (loc. cit. pp. 220-221), "are difficult to force on this point, and that is why an obsession with them, while rarer, is most tenacious, because absolute confidence is more difficult to them. They want to calm their minds with logic: they ask advice and then dispute it; they will walk, but not until they see their way in full light. We know that they will not see it so. Women more readily seek calm of mind in a sentiment of confidence, in the security infused into them by the word of someone whom they may believe. And after all, that also is logical; indeed, it is the only logic that in the circumstances can lead to a conclusion of certitude." Yet, however difficult it may be, the director must gain possession of the scrupulous person's confidence. Without it, no progress can be made towards a cure. Only through confidence in his director will the penitent accept the direction given him, and put it into practice without discussion or argument. So much so, that if with a particular case the director cannot capture the person's full confidence, he must abandon the charge to another who may have better luck.

How can the director inspire this confidence? We give here some general guiding rules which Eymieu (loc. cit.) lays down for the director of a scrupulous penitent.

First of all, you must merit the confidence of the penitent. To some degree you will merit, it, from the start, by the mere fact of your good intentions. Even if you do not see everything clearly, you will see better than the scrupulous person, who is groping in a fog. Were you to offer no more than ordinary commonsense, would not this be a safer guide than a mind obsessed with panic fears and doubts? Then you must convince your penitent that you are fully competent, that you understand his trouble and how to deal with it. You must try to get this into his mind at the outset, in the very first interview. Scrupulous people feel at once an immense desire to be sincere, and an immense difficulty in expounding their case adequately. They are never satisfied, remaining always convinced that they have put their case badly, that they have not told everything, that the minute detail they forgot to mention is perhaps of the highest significance. The result is that they are perpetually retailing the same story, emphasizing now one detail, now another, and finding new matter for doubts at every repetition. This does good neither to the director nor to the penitent himself, so the tendency to repetition must be effectually blocked. How can this be accomplished? The only means is to instill into his mind at the outset, that you have full competence and full understanding of his case. Still, it will be necessary to let the penitent talk freely at first, so that you will be able to remind him afterwards that you have heard the whole statement of his troubles. This statement will be very long, confused, full of useless details. In many cases you will be able, after a few sentences, to direct the account yourself, by putting certain precise and pertinent questions. You must do so with care and kindness, with the unhurried and calm precision of a doctor making a delicate auscultation. The person will usually be surprised and charmed that you have put your finger exactly on the sore spot; he will answer your question and await another. You must seize this advantage, which is already almost a triumph, by applying a list of suitable questions, based on your knowledge of the general nature of scruples, on your personal experience and on your preliminary grasp of the actual case before you. Scruples are so stereotyped in form, that this is not so difficult as it may appear at first sight. Formulate your questions in such a way that your penitent has only to answer, "yes" or "no"—especially "yes." When, during a quarter of an hour, he has had only to answer "yes," when he has seen all his troubles which are hopelessly tangled in his mind, arrange themselves in neat order during the course of your interrogation, all the innumerable and incoherent details sorted out and summarized in a few precise ideas, and when he has felt your exploring finger mark certain points on which he had never before fixed his attention, "There, you suffer in such a manner"—then he will feel an immense relief flooding into his heart; he will feel that he has explained his case well, and been thoroughly understood; above all, he will be ready to place his full confidence in you, disposed to believe in the certainty of cure, if you promise it to him, and to follow the prescription you will give.

It is very useful, even necessary, to impress on the penitent from the start that his is a case of scruples, and that he is not in any way to blame for his doubts and fears. He has committed no sin in the matter which is troubling him; his mental distress is simply a bout of scrupulosity, a hard trial which God sometimes permits, but which he will get over if he does what he is told. This should be simply impressed on his mind, stated clearly in a way suited to his understanding, without any reasoning or argument. Before terminating this first interview, it would be also useful—if the penitent is intelligent and if a further step can be asked of him without causing fatigue—to emphasize the following two points. First, he should be made to understand his principal cause of anguish under some such form as this: "It is impossible for me to make a proper judgment of my own conduct at present; for the time being, I cannot distinguish between right and wrong in my own actions; in the matters which affect me most, I am unable to come to a decision with certainty." Secondly, in a few brief but clear sentences, give him some general explanation of the psychological cause of his scrupulosity, and the general principle of treatment. He may be able, for instance, to grasp the idea that fear and doubt can come from a purely subjective cause, when the mind has been tired by overstrain or by a condition of general ill-health, and that he must now try to reduce his worry by following your directions with simple childlike obedience. The fear and doubt about sin which he feels at present, tell him that he must put it in your hands, that you take full responsibility as a priest.

Give him also every hope of being cured, telling him you will show him the proper way towards complete cure according as he progresses. All this comes down to getting the penitent to accept the fact that he is scrupulous, that a psychological scrupulosity is the cause of all his troubles, that for the moment he sees things in a false light, as it were through colored glasses, and consequently that he will have to surrender himself to be guided by you. And the purpose of all this is not so much to enlighten his understanding as to calm his fears and thus gain his obedience.

If you explain to him briefly and sympathetically the nature of his affliction and how it falsifies his judgment, he will desire to be cured and will take an interest in the treatment. The will to be cured must be inculcated before any treatment, and it should be continually fostered. Therefore, in the course of treatment get him to believe that he is improving. If any improvement shows itself, point this out to him, and keep reminding him of it; every amelioration, however small, must be noted in order to derive encouragement. Show great optimism, and even if progress is imperceptible, tell him that he is improving. You must have, yourself, the strongest faith in the power of religion over the soul, and in the curative power of your direction, a confidence great enough to be communicated spontaneously to your penitent. A strong bond of confidence and sympathy must be established between you. Hence the first interview is often decisive.

As a basis for all this, the director must possess in a high degree the virtue of charity—love of God and of his neighbor, of this neighbor in particular—and in addition a manifest gentleness and kindness which is the bloom of this charity. You should be such that the scrupulous person may feel almost instinctively that he will find security and peace in opening his heart to you, saying to himself: "Here is someone who understands, who is solicitous for my welfare, and takes me seriously." To preserve intact that patience and kindliness with scrupulous people is often difficult, but your sympathy must be so strong as to bear, without the least show of impatience, the obstinacy, the eternal repetitions and absurdities in which they would seem to delight. Yet a want of kindliness at any stage in the process of cure might spoil everything, and bring crashing down the edifice already half built. The scrupulous person is acutely conscious that he is burdensome and irritating to others, and this makes him all the more timidly sensitive to any show of exasperation. The director who is unfalteringly kind will work great good by the atmosphere of calm he sheds around the troubled soul.

To hold fast the confidence of his penitent, the director should, without any false posing, but quite naturally, show himself at every turn equal to his task, and allow the conviction to penetrate that he answers for the good result, provided that the scrupulous person does his share by complete obedience. A certain largeness and flexibility of mind is necessary. Therefore, do not consider it sufficient to have a little set exhortation prepared in advance to be applied indiscriminately to all the scrupulous people whom you may have to direct. General and impersonal arguments can do little to touch a soul which is desirous of direct personal help. Instead of long discourses and clever demonstrations, give clear and concrete decisions, in a few words carefully chosen for the particular time and person. From the start attend to the particular traits of your patient's mind and of his scruples, his character and circumstances of life. Undeterred by his opposition, by his refusal to be convinced, by his seeming lack of sincerity, know how to reaffirm your decisions with unruffled calm.

Gaining and conserving the confidence of the scrupulous person in this way is the first step. The next is to obtain his *obedience*. You must, therefore, be firm, as well as gentle and kind. That firmness will very soon be needed. After having interrogated the penitent once and for all, having heard his whole story sufficiently to inspire his confidence and to make obedience possible and reasonable for him, you must impose silence upon him and forbid any going back over the same account. Similarly, you must cut short any discussion of your decisions and your orders. Of course, account must be taken of an objection of *fact*, for example a circumstance of home life or of duty which prevents the carrying out of your orders, but there must be no *doctrinal* objections allowed; these swarm in the scrupulous mind, and discussion only makes them worse. While docility and obedience are all-important on the part of the scrupulous person, this obedience calls for, on the director's part, an authority capable of evoking it, an authority strong and firm. Any weakness in commanding, or want of firmness in sustaining the order, would certainly provoke disobedience.

Having, as we have said, heard the penitent out, having explained to him briefly and clearly the cause of his scruples, and the necessity he is under of rendering blind obedience to his director, you must end the consultation with a practical prescription to be carried out. Here you must speak plainly, in words that are most precise and not in the least equivocal, in sentences that are short and absolutely clear to the understanding. You must speak categorically: "Do this. Avoid that. I forbid you absolutely to do this or that until further order." Similarly you must beware of putting in conditions such as: "If this occupation should tire you, leave it alone," "If it worries or troubles you, do not do it," "Try, and then you will see what you can do." Any condition of this sort would cause further scruples, and the doubt or hesitation implied would make the penitent conclude that his state was very serious and complex, since even the confessor with all his authority is not able to settle the matter with certainty. You must, therefore, leave no opening for any "ifs" or "perhaps," putting your prescription in a categorical and imperative form. Neither should you give any *reasons* for your decisions as long as the person is incapable, not only of understanding, but of feeling their force in his own case and of being convinced by them with complete certainty. Till then, even the best and clearest reasons will be of no avail to him and will be open doors for new anxieties and doubts. You must above all make sure that he *listens* to you. He will most likely only half listen, with one ear, while he is still seeking in his mind what he has perhaps forgotten to explain. You must ensure that he listens to you with both ears open, and make sure of this by having him repeat the prescription you give him.

Finally, you have to ensure that your orders are put into execution. However wise your prescription is, it will be quite useless unless the scrupulous person puts it into execution, but this is the most difficult as well as the most necessary thing for him. He will inevitably fight shy of it, but you must not allow him any means of escape. Employ every device to make him put your orders into practice; tell him, for instance, that you will have nothing more to say to him until he has executed the orders just given to him.

To maintain your necessary authority over him, you must never *reverse* your decisions or change your opinions. The person must feel that your decisions are oracular utterances, unchangeable, absolutely trustworthy. Then, however clear, peremptory and well-understood your prescription has been, you must realize that you will have to repeat it frequently. It would not be firmness, but an error of tactics and of psychological method to tell him that you will not repeat your orders. Such repetition when you have made yourself quite clear and been understood, may be illogical, but there is more than logic in man, and you must remember that it is not enough for the scrupulous person to understand and to determine here and now that he will execute your orders; his will is sick more than his intellect and needs to be constantly supported. The directions which he has received from you will gradually lose their precision and their force with the mere passage of time. His will must be recharged like an accumulator.

The function of the person directed is to obey, not through force but freely. To obey is his manner of being reasonable and free—reasonable because he thus escapes from his torturing doubts; free, because he thus dominates his impressions and recovers his personality. The scrupulous person spontaneously desires to render this obedience, just as he seeks to be directed, but he will be very inclined to divide up the directions he has been given and to follow only part of them. He must be pressed to render an obedience which is complete and entire, or your prescription will avail nothing. All or nothing is the rule; there must be no share left to the obsessing scruples. A child, when being taught to pray, on coming to this part, "My God, I give You all that I have," stopped suddenly and added in a low voice, "except my little rabbit." If the scrupulous person persists in keeping to himself against obedience his little rabbit, he will soon find himself in a worse state than ever. He can be told that unless he gives you total obedience, which is the sole and indispensable means of cure, you will only have to relinquish the charge altogether. Even when convinced of the necessity of complete obedience, the scrupulous person will find it difficult in practice, because it goes against the strong current of all his fears and troubled ideas. You can help him in this by fostering in his mind a strong, absolute, unfaltering desire to be cured.

All the foregoing directions may appear rather complicated, and it may appear at first sight very difficult for a director of souls to keep in mind so many important rules when dealing with a scrupulous penitent. That is because the right approach is so important in this matter. It is very easy to make a wrong beginning in treating a case of scruples, and a wrong beginning here is extremely difficult to set right afterwards. Again, we have tried to put down clearly the general rules which should guide the director, not only on the first occasion, but in all his interviews with the scrupulous person. The theory will inevitably be more complicated than the actual practice. There must be nothing complicated, of course, in the actual treatment of the scrupulous person. He should be given very simple, easy directions in a straightforward manner, and on any one occasion he should be given no more than he is ready to assimilate. It would be better for the director to err on the side of brevity, than to give a lot of complicated advice and explanations which, if remembered at all by the penitent, would only be misinterpreted or misapplied. It may easily be found, for example, that on the first occasion the penitent can be given no more than the simple idea that he is a case of scrupulosity, and that he must come back again for advice to the same confessor.

So far we have been speaking only of the general form of treatment, of the manner in which the director should give advice and direction to the scrupulous penitent. We have now to describe what this direction will be.

Scrupulosity, we have seen, manifests itself in the mind as an inability to form practical definite judgments with regard to some moral precept. The theoretical precept is clear and definite to the scrupulous person, but he finds an insuperable difficulty in applying it to his own case. His thought will take some such form as this: "I am strictly forbidden to receive Holy Communion in the state of mortal sin; but perhaps I have committed a grave sin since my last Confession; I can't be sure; therefore I can't make up my mind whether or not to go to Holy Communion." How can the scrupulous person be helped over this difficulty? The difficulty will always be the same, no matter what the subject-matter of the scruples may be, namely, it will be the difficulty of applying the general precept to the person's own acts. His psychical force is not equal to the task, so the difficulty must be reduced by giving the scrupulous person the following rule of conduct, which he must firmly hold and apply in every case of doubt:

For me, in all matters of conscience, whether of venial or of mortal sin, it is only complete certainty that counts.

Or it may be formulated as follows:

I am guilty of a sin, mortal or venial, only when I am completely certain.

The scrupulous person must clearly understand and grasp this rule in order to apply it to the solving of every anxious doubt. Thus:

For me: not true, perhaps, for others, but for me. I can, I should, and I want to obey this rule; it is the prescription, so I have only to follow it exactly.

In all matters of conscience: hence in all possible cases where it is my concern to avoid sin, whether venial or mortal. Hence, if I am not certain that an act is a sin, it is not a sin. If I am certain that it is sinful, but not certain that it is a mortal sin, it is then only a venial sin.

It is only complete certainty that counts: that is, a certainty in my own mind which excludes all possible doubt, all appearance of error; a certainty which is calm, full, as clear as two plus two equals four; so certain that I am incapable of doubting it. And since only this certainty counts, I must not care about the rest; these "perhaps," these fears mean that I am not certain, so I despise them, I pass over them, I act as if they did not exist.

Notice that this rule is not expressed in the past tense, but in the present. It is infallible in the present, and that suffices. You live in the present, therefore leave the past alone; your duty is concerned only with the present; your duty is to sanctify the present. "But perhaps I am not in the state of grace." If you are not, the only way to recover it is to do what God asks of you here and now. Leave the past alone, for it is finished; leave the future, for it has not yet come; only the present is your concern what you have to do. And what you have to do now is to go forward, holding to the rule of conduct given to you. For there will be only one of two things: either you will have complete certainty that you are violating an obligation, that you are committing a sin, or you will not have this clear certainty. If you have you will see it quite clearly, for complete certainty means that you have not the least doubt. If you are not completely certain whether it is sinful, then whatever you do, you are doing right—not only are you not committing the least fault, but you are doing a good thing, because you are doing your duty generously, acting against your anxieties and fears, and curing yourself of your scruples.

This rule is summed up in the word: "Go ahead, unless

you are absolutely certain of sin." For the scrupulous person this rule is absolute, there are no exceptions to it, and no additions to be made to it. It is also legitimate, wherever scrupulosity is concerned, for given the state of mind of the scrupulous person, he will never fail to see any sin clearly, when it is a reality. There is no more chance of the scrupulous person taking a sin to be a lawful act, than there is of the miser mistaking a burglar for a friend calling in for a chat. We are here assuming, of course, that the doubts in question are *scrupulous* doubts, for the rule given is the privilege only of scrupulous people, and in those matters alone in which they are scrupulous. This must not cause any difficulty in practice, however, for then the very purpose of the privilege would be defeated. Those whose scruples are very chronic, and whose minds are constantly obsessed by them, can be told simply to apply the rule of absolute certainty to *all* doubts that disturb their conscience. Others may be scrupulous to a less acute degree, and in only one more or less clearly circumscribed subject-matter. These again should be given the rule without restriction, lest by throwing the responsibility on them of deciding in practice what is a scrupulous doubt, and what a simple prudent doubt, the way be left open to fresh anxieties. The only restriction, therefore, applies in practice to the director, in that he must avoid the mistake of judging a priori, without consideration, that every question of the scrupulous person implies a scruple, and of brushing aside every doubt that is put to him for solution. Scrupulous penitents, like every one else, sometimes have simple and ordinary doubts and errors, which must be corrected by truth in a straightforward way. In case of doubt as to the scrupulous origin, the rule still applies: only complete certainty counts. The scrupulous person, therefore, must be given complete security in the application of the rule of conduct given to him; he must be confident that he may and should apply it to conquering all his anxious doubts without exception.

The rule is efficacious. On the one hand, it is very simple and falls within the psychological power of the scrupulous mind. It is much easier to say, "I am not absolutely certain that this act is sinful," than to say, "I am absolutely certain it is a good action." Secondly, the effect directly produced by applying the rule is to suppress all anxious inquiry, all torturing doubts. These were produced by the vain effort of seeking an impossible certainty, and the source of this struggle is now removed. Naturally the rule is efficacious only if it is applied in practice by the scrupulous person. The director must make sure that it is understood and accepted as a working principle, and then actually applied. Most women and many men penitents pay little attention to it at first, and are unconcerned about it, becoming bored when the director insists on it. They incline rather to seize on a word which gives momentary relief, like "Don't worry," "Remain tranquil in your mind." They delight in such practical commands, which give balm—for the moment—but in this they delude themselves, for although freed from their anxiety of the moment, they will presently experience a hundred others, and before they reach home they will feel the need of returning for another dose of the tranquilizing balm, which soothes for a little while but cures nothing. The director's task, like that of every educator, is to make himself unneeded, to teach the scrupulous person to walk by himself, to live his own life; by degrees, therefore, he must be got to apply the saving rule and solve his own scruples by his own efforts.

Such is the general rule of conduct to be given to all those troubled with scruples. It is the rule given by moralists in general, and in explaining it, we have followed, more or less exactly, the formulation of it given so clearly by Eymieu *(Le gouvernement de soi-meme. II. L'Obsession et le Scruple)*. A director will know by his experience and common sense, and by his knowledge of the particular case he has to treat, the best manner of giving this rule in practice.

We give now, very briefly, a few practical examples of applying the rule of certainty, in particular cases of scruples which are of frequent occurrence. Any one penitent afflicted by scruples will, until such time as a cure is effected, constantly present the same class of doubts., The answer will always be the same: a repetition of the practical rule. This repetition has the salutary effect of reinforcing it in the person's mind, and of convincing him of its universal application and efficacy.

The Sacrament of Confession is the occasion of several kinds of scruples. Docile obedience to the confessor will simplify the difficulty. The penitent should be clearly instructed that he is obliged to confess only sins which are *certainly* mortal, and *certainly* committed—with grave matter, full advertance, full consent. If there is any doubt on any one of these points, there is no need to confess it, for only absolute certainty counts. If at the moment of Confession he is not absolutely certain of a mortal sin, then there is nothing that he is bound to confess; he is free to confess any venial sin, and his confession is good.

The preparatory examination of conscience can be a torture, some scrupulous people spending hours at it without being satisfied, and the confessor should prescribe for these some fixed limit of time, say one or two minutes, or even allow no examination at all. Many will strive to confess explicitly each and every venial sin, and it will be necessary to limit them to a prescribed number of accusations, for instance two or three at most. Again it must be repeated: "ifs" and "perhaps" do not count, only absolute certainty.

The Treatment of Scruples

With regard to the question of a general confession, it may sometimes be more prudent to accede to the desire of a scrupulous person to make one, when it is foreseen that it may bring some satisfaction to his mind. The confessor should himself interrogate briefly in this case and direct the course of the accusations, finally reassuring the penitent that he has made a good confession, that all and everything is now forgiven, and that he must never go back on the past again. Having once allowed a general confession, it will be easier to refuse any further requests for a repetition, and any doubts about a previous confession must be immediately conquered by applying the practical rule: doubts must be despised, only certainty matters.

When the time comes to receive Holy Communion, scruples frequently arise from the fear of having broken the fast, or of not being in the state of grace. Here our rule has a clear application. The scrupulous person must be told: "Unless you are absolutely sure, without the least doubt, that you have broken your fast, go to Communion." "But if, in fact, I have broken my fast?" "Then you are dispensed." Similarly, "Unless you are absolutely certain, without any doubt, that you are in mortal sin, go to Communion." "But suppose that in fact I am not in the state of grace?" "Then Communion will put you in the state of grace." In some such way all arguments should be cut short.

Scrupulous persons of strict purity are frequently obsessed by impure imaginings. The fact that they are really scrupulous with regard to these impure thoughts is a sign that they are not temptations, and that any sin is unlikely to be committed there, for the current of their will is running strongly in the contrary direction. Our rule applies again here, and it can be expressed in the following manner. During the crisis: do not consent, that is all—no grimaces, no nerve-twisting, no expressions of distaste, no imprecations against the devil, no prayers even, nothing—because any of these only tend to fix your imagination on these images, creating mental associations and habits. After the crisis: do not examine your conscience (for the same reasons,) and provided that you do not see with complete certainty straightaway, without examination, in spite of yourself, that you have committed a mortal sin (again full advertence and full consent), which will probably never happen, do not worry, but go about your business in peace. With regard to this point of impure images in the mind, scrupulous persons can be helped a great deal by being assured that they are not to blame for their imaginations, that their very anxiety shows that they don't want these bad thoughts, and that even the saints were troubled in the same way.

Devotions of obligation can give occasion to many scruples. It may be the penance prescribed in Confession, the hearing or the saying of Mass, the saying of the Divine Office, or other duties. The person will be tortured by doubt as to whether he has the requisite intention, or whether on account of involuntary distraction during the prayer he has really fulfilled his obligation, and he will make interminable repetitions of the same prayer without ever attaining the desired certainty. The confessor should energetically combat such weaknesses, and he should insist gently, but quite firmly, on his penitent applying the practical rule: "Unless you are absolutely certain that you have said the prayer wrongly, you are under no further obligation, you have done all that God wants." Such persons should never be allowed to repeat their prayers of obligation; for instance, the scrupulous priest should be put under obedience never to repeat a part of his Divine Office, never to repeat or even to stop short while saying Mass. Nothing so exposes to distractions and to further doubts, as the thought that prayers may be repeated after they have been said badly. Let such a practice be begun, and it will soon become habitual, since the repetition will be attended by no better success than the first attempts. The scrupulous person must be taught not to exact more of himself than does God, to Whom his humility and obedience here will be more pleasing.

The scrupulous person will not fail to put forward all kinds of objections. The confessor must not fall into the snare of entering into an argument. It sometimes seems that a little clear reasoning would solve the doubts and difficulties of scrupulous people, but this is an illusion, for they are suffering from too much, not too little reasoning The only way to answer their objections is by repeating the rule of conduct, and this is also a practical way of making it understood and driving it home. Thus they say: "I am not scrupulous; I have not been frank; I forgot to mention a whole lot of things; you think too highly of me; I have explained myself badly; you have not understood me." All these are only "perhaps," further doubts and scruples, and the director should answer: "It is not according to what you told me, but what I *know*, motu proprio, that I give you this rule of conduct. Besides, for you it is only complete certainty that counts."

"But, supposing I understand or apply this rule badly, if I give it too wide an interpretation?" "Only absolute certainty counts. Unless you are certain that you are misapplying it, go ahead. You cannot misapply it; whatever interpretation you give it is good, as long as it is not *certainly* forbidden."

"But I read such a book, I heard such a sermon, in which the opposite was said—at least I think so."—"That is not certainty, and even if you were certain of what you read or heard, it would not be clearly evident that it was for you. Your rule is this..."

"But I never know when I am quite certain."—"Then you never are certain. When you are certain, you will know it perfectly, without any doubt."

Scrupulosity, as we have seen, is usually concerned with some one class of moral judgments, some one precept or virtue. It is fear of sin in this matter which constitutes the scrupulous person's greatest difficulty, and the rule of conduct we have described, the rule of certainty, aims directly at reducing this particular difficulty. There may sometimes be secondary difficulties, in the form of lesser scruples, or errors, or simple doubts, and according as these appear, they must be treated according to need, due account, of course, being taken of the person's character and of his degree of psychological strength available. If the secondary trouble is caused simply by an erroneous idea, the only cure is to correct the error by stating the truth. This may call for some discussion and reasoning with the penitent—a manner of treatment which can never be used for real scruples, but which will be applicable here in proportion as the error is not directly related to the point of the scrupulosity. In some cases of simple error, the director's authority will be necessary to make the truth accepted, and if doubts still persist, the penitent must cling to obedience, acting as if conviction were absolute.

A number of errors regarding moral obligations are of frequent occurrence among lay people, and these errors can increase greatly the mental trouble of the scrupulous. As soon as the scrupulous person's chief anxiety and fear begins to lessen appreciably, any error must be corrected by a short and clear exposition of the truth. The following are a few explanations, without detailed qualification, of some frequent errors:

1) We are not obliged to avoid absolutely every *occasion* of

sin, still less every occasion of indeliberate bad thoughts. We cannot avoid every occasion of sin as long as we live on this earth. Often we have to apply the principle of the double effect, and permit an occasion of evil. Only a good and clear conscience can find exact measure here.

2) Positive precepts, imposing an act to be performed, do not oblige absolutely, but only when the act is morally and physically possible, and not when there is a proportionately grave excuse. God cannot ask the impossible. For instance, assistance at Mass on Sunday is not obligatory when there is danger to health in going out.

3) The more perfect in theory is not always the more perfect in practice or the more perfect for you. All circumstances must be taken into account, especially the circumstance of scrupulosity. Duty comes before counsel, and the first duty of a scrupulous person is to get cured.

4) Every pain is not good, nor every pleasant thing bad. Virtue is sometimes a pleasure; and God often wants us to do things which we like doing, and which bring pleasure to ourselves.

5) An idea is not an act of the will; an intention, and the most monstrous thoughts can arise in the mind without a perverse inclination of the will. An idea or imagination can give pleasure spontaneously, but there is no sin except by a free act of the will.

6) A scrupulous, doubtful conscience is not a sign of any sinful movement in the will. On the contrary, a real scruple is usually a sign of strong opposition of the will.

7) A temptation, however strong, is not a sin. The Evil One tempted even the Son of God.

8) You are bound to confess only the mortal sins you re-

member. Again, God does not ask the impossible. Confession is Christ's merciful way of healing the wounds of sin, and therefore we can be sure that Confession has nothing very complicated or very difficult in it. Of course, your sorrow for mortal sin must be universal. A forgotten sin, never confessed, is forgiven with the rest in a good Confession. This is a point of frequent confusion of thought. For one thing, you cannot make a bad Confession by mistake, or through lapse of memory, and a good Confession takes away all grave sins. Then again, there is quite a distinct difference between the forgiveness of a sin and the obligation of confessing it.

A distinction that is frequently not grasped by scrupulous people (and by others) is that between feeling and consenting. It causes them many difficulties, and it must be made clear to them, when necessary, by some simple example, such as the following suggested by Eymieu—"Suppose that a spoonful of pepper is put on your tongue, and that you are immediately gagged; it tastes very unpleasant, you feel it, and you don't consent to it. Now imagine that a spoonful of sugar is placed on your tongue and you are then gagged; you taste it and like it, and no doubt, you consent to it. But suppose you are told that the sugar is poisoned, what then? You still feel the sweetness, and you can't help liking it, but you don't want it, you don't consent to it, and you will spit it out, however sweet it is, as soon as the gag falls from your mouth. Similarly, when your mind is disturbed by temptations or bad thoughts, they often taste pleasant, and you can't help that, but your very agitation, your fears, your anxious doubts mean that you don't consent at all."

It will also be necessary to reduce the difficulty caused by exaggerated desires in the matter of virtue, in particular the desire for absolute or mathematical certitude that one is in the state of grace, or that one is doing the better thing in a particular circumstance. Scrupulous people must be taught that human life has to proceed without this absolute certitude, that we are human and not divine, and that God wants us to do our present duty without vainly striving to see, to feel, to be certain of things that are beyond us. Life comes before logic. How often is it not forgotten that hope is one of the great theological virtues! The example may be quoted of St. Joan of Arc: "If I am in the state of grace, may God deign to keep me there; if I am not, may He deign to put me in it." Then again, scrupulous people are to realize that they are sick—a hard fact—and there are many desires within the powers of a healthy person which the sick person must agree to forego until he is cured. He must ask less of himself, using prudent economy of desire, of sentiment, of effort, even in matters of virtue and the pursuit of perfection. Once again, he is driven to docile obedience as his present rule of life. His director will have to judge what acts, for instance an intellectual study which has become too hard for the moment, are simply impossible or relatively unnecessary, and will have to be omitted for a time. Still, the person must lead a normal life, as far as possible, hence nothing reasonable or necessary should be omitted, such as prayer and the sacraments, but made easier.

Reducing the difficulty of the psychological act, in the manner described in the preceding pages, goes a long way towards curing scruples, and it spontaneously induces a raising of the psychological tension. This will often be found to be sufficient, in cases where scrupulosity has not reached a very acute stage. With other sufferers, treatment must be pushed a further step. There are two ways in which this must be done:

avoiding waste of psychical energy, and directly increasing the psychical force.

Life is increased by exercise; that is one of its laws, but one which applies only within certain limits, too much use or too little having the contrary effect. A muscle grows and develops through exercise. If over-exercised, however, until fatigue becomes greater than the powers of recuperation, the result will be strain, more or less permanent according to the extent to which the limit has been exceeded. The same law applies in the psychological field of our activity, for although our psychological energy has natural powers of recuperation from fatigue, mental strain will result from exceeding the safe limit. The normal routine of our life makes demands upon our psychical energy, and a balance must be struck between supply and demand, if we are to preserve our mental health and strength. People afflicted with scruples, we have seen, have too low a level of psychical tension to meet the demands made upon it, and in consequence they are in a constant state of mental strain. To reduce this strain, certain measures must be taken.

Prevention. To avoid muscle strain, we must do two things. We must take enough physical exercise to develop our muscles up to normal requirements and we must avoid overworking them beyond the reasonable limit. It is well known that the health of the body reacts upon that of the mind and vice versa. It is not surprising, therefore, that scrupulosity, which is a state of low mental vitality, affects to some extent the physical well-being. Scrupulous people need a reasonable amount both of physical and mental exercise, and they frequently need direction in this matter, so as to avoid the extremes of too much and too little. Owing to their general depression, those who are more chronically afflicted by scruples tend rather to inactivity, below that required for health. Common sense will be easily able to fix the amount of physical exercise for them. Their mental activity, being less tangible, is not so easy to regulate, and here their tendency is often towards excess. The scrupulous person has to use economy with his restricted psychical energy.

As regards physical activity, and to a certain extent also mental work. The following is a good general rule. If you feel tired at the beginning of an action, pay no attention to your apparent fatigue; carry on, and it will often disappear. If, however, you feel tired after you have continued an activity for some time, and this fatigue increases with the continuation of the activity, you should stop.

To eliminate mental strain in particular, the scrupulous person must avoid, as best as he can, all thinking and ruminating on his anxious doubts and all dispersal of mind over ideas associated with them. Let him apply his thought at every moment rather to the external work in which he is engaged. He must be careful to withdraw his mind from too prolonged an application to one subject. Reflection, study, reading, in a word all intellectual activity, although beneficial and necessary, must be interrupted or varied from time to time, for mental strain is nearly always the result of too prolonged an application to the same work. When the brain cells are denied their periods of recuperation, psychical energy is being squandered.

A more disastrous waste of psychical energy is involved in overindulgence of emotions and sentiments. Above all, scrupulous people need to avoid moods of sadness: ennui, melancholy, mental anguish, dark sorrows, depression, torpor, discouragement, moral prostration. All these are evil signs and become agents of evil. They are the conscious signs of the loss of harmony and mental dislocation produced by scruples, but to surrender oneself to these feelings means a further slackening of the spring of life. All depressive sadness, therefore, must be courageously resisted.

Repair. Rest, as a period of recuperation, is a physical necessity of nature. Scrupulous people, since their mental affliction involves an extra drain on their capital of energy, will need more rest than the normal. This extra rest should not, however, be absolute, for such a remedy would often be worse than the disease, favoring the development of morbid thoughts. In general, it is more beneficial to multiply short periods of rest in such a way that the person may not require any very long rest periods, and even in cases where a prolonged continuous rest is necessary, it is better to occupy the time quietly and easily with small tasks that are varied and agreeable rather than to do nothing. Distractions are another kind of mental rest often beneficial, but there are good and bad distractions. Many people depressed by scruples seek relief in the exhilaration of exciting amusements, but this kind does them little good. They should be directed rather to distractions that are calming, peaceful, and healthy, and which do not require to be taken in strictly measured doses, as for example, the exhilaration of a walk in the fresh country air.

Mental strain squanders the capital of psychical energy, moderate activity of the right kind will increase it. To increase this capital of life, which is to augment the psychological power of unification, we must develop little by little the functions which are below the norm, using a treatment measured according to the actual state of the person, and to the actual amount of psychical energy at his disposal. Many systems of such practical exercises are advocated, and in general it may be said of them that all are good if employed intelligently. The personal qualities of the director, devotedness, experience, flair, tact, these are of more account than the particular system of exercises used.

We give here in broad outline some general exercises which will be found useful. They must be varied and adapted according to the infinite varieties of *cases*. The first exercises may seem very elementary, but they will be necessary in the more chronic cases of scrupulosity.[1]

1) *Conscious Acts:* These exercises consist simply in deliberately taking consciousness of what you are doing. "I am moving this arm, my head, my eyes; I am walking, I am listening, I am hearing, I am looking at this picture, this view," etc. The consciousness of the scrupulous person is often somnolent, distracted, or else it is all hazy and confused. These easy exercises, prescribed for some minutes each day at fixed hours, excite his consciousness, concentrate it and increase its power of unification.

2) *Voluntary Acts:* This is a further step. Instead of just taking deliberate cognizance, you deliberately will to do some act. What act? Any simple act, and merely as an exercise of the will. "I will to raise my arm, to walk, to go here, to look there, to move this object, to shut this door," and so on. These exercises may be prescribed, for example, to be performed three times each morning; three determined movements of the arms, then six, then twelve, by a free effort of the will.

3) *Exercises of Concentration:* These condense the two preceding exercises. Write a number, for example the number 1, or 4. See it, hear it in your imagination, be conscious of the movements of your fingers in writing it. Then shut your eyes, and continue to think of the number as long as you can with-

---

[1] Note: These exercises will be found described in more detail in Eymieu, loc. cit., in Arnaud d'Agnel et d'Espiney, *Le Scrupule*, and in other books.

out distraction. Or else you can represent to yourself an external object or one of your fingers. The essential point is to apply your mind deliberately to some object which is quite simple, material and concrete, which can scarcely evoke any associations of ideas, so that it will be easier to keep away all distraction. This exercise is very efficacious. It gathers together the dispersed consciousness, drawing it closer and making its unity stronger. For healthy people it is a good preparation for concentrated, intellectual work, and for those afflicted with scrupulosity it is a beneficial exercise if performed from time to time during the day.

4) *Exercises of Attention:* The function of attention is of capital importance, for it is essentially an act of the will. Being particularly reduced in the scrupulous mind, efforts must be made to restore it to normal level. Although the preceding exercises improve the act of attention, something more can be done. The principal means is work—a physical, intellectual, or artistic work, suitably chosen and graduated. The work should be interesting, whether in itself or from any added circumstance, so that the person can the more easily apply his attention to it. It should not be too difficult nor too prolonged, in order to avoid strain and failure, but just difficult enough to require a small effort of attention. Games, such as tennis, are useful, especially if the person is not yet proficient, for then he must apply his attention more deliberately. On the whole, however, some serious work is preferable, since it captures the attention more profoundly, and better attaches the action to the personality. Any intellectual task has the advantage of being easy to graduate in relation to the powers and energy of each particular person. With reading, for example, a single page or chapter can be read, then repeated either orally or in writing; after some time a longer passage can be taken and a longer

interval interposed between reading and repetition. With regard to artistic work, music practice is often too difficult or fatiguing; drawing and painting are better, for those with the talent, for they require a calm and sustained attention which is not exhausting.

The person oppressed by scrupulosity will have various objections to these occupations, even to those that are easy, for scrupulous persons often become apathetic and moody. They will have little relish for any kind of activity, saying that they are not interested, whatever is suggested to them, be it even sport, distraction, or amusement. They must be induced and brought to the resolution of giving themselves over to the prescribed occupation, even with enthusiasm, as if they were keen on it, as if they were interested. That small initial *effort* will often purchase them an hour of strength, and their appetite will be aroused when they deliberately overcome the inertia.

The director will find that a prescribed order of time for the day is almost indispensable for performing these exercises. Left to his personal initiative, the person would not find the energy for the many small decisions to be made, against which a hundred objections would arise in his mind at every moment. The order of time should be broad enough not to encumber him with additional tortures, but definite enough to leave no room for uncertainty, sufficiently imperative to remove all hesitation. Fidelity to this timetable will be an additional exercise for his consciousness, will, attention, and general effort. Finally he can be advised to fix for himself a timetable for his daily and weekly duties.

The culminating point of all these exercises is *decision,* just as indecision is the characteristic mark of the mind obsessed with scruples. By bringing oneself to making small decisions, one acquires the habit of mental decision. It is not enough to say to the scrupulous person: "Decide, make up your mind"; you must decide for him at first, then lead him to make small decisions of little consequence without worrying whether he has made the better choice.

In many cases, of course, a spiritual director is not in a position to advocate or explain these psychological exercises to the scrupulous person. Nor are they ever essential in order to obtain a complete cure of scrupulosity. We have included them here, very briefly in order to bring out even more clearly the nature of scrupulosity as a general psychological weakness. Soul and body, nature and supernatural, make one in the living person. Scrupulosity in particular is an ailment which frequently needs a doctor as well as a priest.

In conclusion, let us emphasize the aid and consolation which religion can give to the scrupulous. If we have seemed to disregard this important factor in our description of the treatment of scruples, that has been because our preoccupation was merely with the psychological aspect of scruples, taking it for granted that every confessor and director of souls will know the inestimable value of prayer, Penance and the Holy Eucharist for the cure of scruples.

APPENDIX

Scruple (Lat. *Scrupulus*, "a small sharp, pointed, stone", hence, in a transferred sense, "uneasiness of mind"), an unfounded apprehension and consequently unwarranted fear that something is a sin, which, as a matter of fact, is not. It is not considered here so much as an isolated act, but rather as a habitual state of mind known to directors of "a scrupulous conscience." St. Alphonsus describes it as a condition in which one, influenced by trifling reasons, and without any solid foundation, is often afraid that sin lies where it really does not. This anxiety may be entertained not only with regard to what is to be done presently, but also with regard to what has been done. The idea sometimes obtaining that scrupulosity is in itself a spiritual benefit of some sort, is, of course, a great error. The providence of God permits it and can gather good from it as from other forms of evil. That apart, however, it is a bad habit doing harm, sometimes grievously, to body and soul. Indeed, persisted in with the obstinacy characteristic of persons who suffer from this malady, it may entail the most lamentable consequences. The judgment is seriously warped, the moral power out in futile combat, and then not unfrequently the scrupulous person makes shipwreck of salvation either on the Scylla of despair or the Charybdis of unheeding indulgence in vice.

It is of great importance to be able to make a correct diagnosis of this disease. Hence especially guides of consciences should be familiar with the symptoms that betray its presence as well as with the causes which commonly give rise to it. For one thing, the confessor should not confound a delicate with a scrupulous conscience, neither should he interpret the reasonable solicitude sometimes discernible in those who are trying to emerge from a life of sin as a sign of scrupulosity. Then, too, ordinarily he ought not to hastily reach this conclusion on the very first experience of his penitent. It is true there are cases of scruples which may be recognized from the start, but this is not the rule. Some special indications that persons are really scrupulous, generally adopted by theologians, are those enumerated by Lacroix. Among these is a certain rooted attachment to their own opinion which makes them unwilling to abide by the judgment of those whom they consult, even though these latter have every title to deference. In consequence, they go from one confessor to another, change their convictions with hardly a shadow of motive, and are tortured by an overshadowing dread that sin lurks in everything they do, and say, and think. The scrupulous may, and ought to, act in defiance of their misgivings, i.e., against their so-called conscience. Nor can they, therefore, be impeached as acting in a state of practical doubt. The unreal phantasm that affrights their imagination, or the unsubstantial consideration that offers itself to their disturbed reason, has no validity against the conscience once formed upon the pronouncement of the confessor or in some other equally trustworthy fashion. In the various perplexities as to the lawfulness of their actions they are not bound to employ any such scrutiny as would be incumbent upon persons in a normal condition. They are not bound to repeat anything of former confessions unless they are sure, without protracted examination, that it is a mortal sin and has never been properly confessed.

Their chief remedy is, having reposed confidence in some confessor, to obey his decisions and commands entirely and absolutely. They are counseled also to avoid idleness, and thus to close the avenue of approach to the wild conjectures and

APPENDIX

strange ponderings responsible for so many of their worries. They should remove the cause of their scruples in so far as it may have been of their own choosing. Hence they are to guard against the reading of ascetical books of a rigorist trend and any intercourse with those afflicted in the same way as themselves. If the source of their scruples be ignorance—for example, with regard to the obligation of some commandment—they are to be instructed, discretion being used in the imparting of the necessary information. If it be a propensity to melancholy, certain harmless pleasures and rational enjoyments may be employed with advantage. Confessors to whom falls the difficult task of receiving the confessions of these harassed souls are to carefully inquire into the origin of the anxieties laid before them. They are to treat their unhappy penitents in general with great kindness. Occasionally, however, some degree of severity may be useful when the penitent shows an extreme tenacity in adhering to his own unreasonable view of the situation. As a rule, the confessor's answers to the innumerable troubles submitted should be clear, unaccompanied by reasons, and so unhesitating as to inspire courage. He should not permit the presentation indefinitely of the various doubts, much less, of course, the repetition of past confessions. Finally, he may sometimes do what should hardly ever be done in any other instance, that is, forbid the penitent to have recourse to another confessor.

Slater, *Manual of Moral Theology* (New York 1908); St. Alphonsus Liguori, *Theologia moralis* (Turin 1888); Genicot, *Theologiae moralis institutiones* (Louvain, 1898); Ballerini, *Opus theologicum morale* (Prato, 1898).

—The Catholic Encyclopedia, 1908